# Too Far, Yet Too Close

RAHAT BHATIA

# Contents


Acknowledgments ................................................ vii

1. A Guy and A Girl ............................................. 1

2. Its Been A Long Time ......................................... 5

3. Imagination .................................................. 8

4. Your Touch .................................................. 13

5. If I Go ..................................................... 16

6. Friday Night ................................................ 23

7. Rain ........................................................ 25

8. Since You Left .............................................. 27

9. Can I Be Him? ............................................... 30

10. Long Walks ................................................. 34

11. Please Don't Say ........................................... 36

12. I'd Be Lying ............................................... 39

13. You're Not There ........................................... 42

14. If He Cries ................................................ 45

15. Old Friends ................................................ 48

16. Is It Just Me? ............................................. 50

17. What We Had ................................................ 53

18. The Dog I Never Had ........................................ 55

19. Would You? ................................................. 57

20. Alright .................................................... 60

21. The Flower In Your Hair .................................... 62

# CONTENTS


22. The Cliff ........................................................... 64

23. A Girl In The Coffe Shop ...................................... 67

24. How Could Someone Not Like Rain ................................. 69

25. A Drive Alone ..................................................... 72

# Acknowledgments

In addition to dedication and determination, creating a book also need the assistance and support of people around you. As I grasp the pages of my very first poetry book, I am very grateful to the people who made my dream come true.

Firstly, I would like to express my heartfelt gratitude to my family. Your unwavering belief in me and your never-ending support kept me going, even when doubt started to creep in. I dedicate my book to you since I was inspired by your affection.

I'd like to thank my friends and peers, my supporters, and for being understanding of my excitement for giving ears to my words. The gratitude I feel for your support is beyond words.

I have an obligation of appreciation to all writers, poets, and artists whose works have had an impact on me. Your creativity sparked my own, and I'm glad i could be a part of such a diverse artistic community.

Finally yet importantly, I would want to thank the readers. It means the world to me that you are reading my thoughts and are eager to go on this lyrical adventure. I hope you have a particular place in your hearts for my poems.

I would like to express my gratitude to everyone whose names I've disclosed as well as to everyone who has supported me silently. This book belongs to each of us equally.


With heartfelt gratitude,

Rahat Bhatia

# 1. A Guy and A Girl

I saw a guy and a girl walking,

Eyes in eyes, they were talking.


5'11" was the guy,

And the girl was 5'4" tall.

Once upon a time,

This was 'Us' after all.


I was driving in a hurry,

So, they both went blurry.


With his hand on her shoulder,

He seemed to be older.


She was with her untied hair,

And he was in a different heart affair.

I thought to stop and start to imagine,

Because in reality, it's hard for me to win.


She was a little shy,

But with him, she asked herself, 'Why?'


They were not at all afraid,

Each other's heart they used to raid.


I wish they just don't end,

Because I know it hurts to be a friend.


The way she folded her arms,

Showed her her fear.

But to overcome,

She had him near.

I think it was You and Me,

Because some time back, this is what we used to be.

3

Today, I saw a guy and a girl walking,

Just like we used to be talking...

Just like we used to be gawking...

# 2. Its Been a Long Time

It's been a long time,

Since I felt your smile.

It's been a long time,

Since we walked a mile.


It's been a long time,

To feel your touch.

It's been a long time,

A quite too much.


It's been a long time,

To feel your hair.

It's been a long time,

When love was in the air.


It's been a long time,

To look into your eyes.

It's been a long time,

To look at the night skies.

It's been a long time,

And I am tired of this wait.

It's been a long time,

Since we tested our fate.

It's been a long time,

To share our tears.

It's been a long time,

To face our fears.

It's been a long time

To feel you by my side.

It's been a long time,

When I used to confide.

It's been a long time,

To share our hearts under stars.

It's been a long time,

Since we healed our scars.


It's been a long time,

To feel loved about.

It's been a long time

When we drink and shout.


It's been a long time,

To feel strong together.

It's been a long time,

To enjoy the weather.


It's been a long time dear,

And I've missed you.

In all my dreams,

I've just wished you...

# 3. Imagination

It's raining outside,

And I am sitting in the dark.

In my imagination,

I can hear your doggy bark.


Sometimes the clouds, they lighten,

And if you were here, my hug would tighten.


Soft songs turned on,

Making it all the more romantic.

And we close our eyes,

Where in there is no public.


In some light,

I can see the raindrops falling.

At the same time,

Giving life to some tadpoles crawling.

I am sitting in a 'House',

But my heart stuck at my 'Home'.

No one's to hear me,

I am all alone.


No one's to talk to me,

And I miss you all the more.

Even the phone calls don't work,

I need you in person, hardcore.


This rain has got that nostalgic smell,

Telling me that you're well.


I need you tonight, to talk to me, careless,

In this solitude, my heart is carrying regrets.


Alone in this rain, I read my book,

But if you were here to eat, I'd cook.

I have got prolonged days and even longer nights,

And my heart sleeps with your reminiscing sights.

# 4. Your Touch

Your touch was,

As soft as a flower.

I'm drowning in that feeling,

And can't get over.


Your soft tender skin,

Rubbed against mine.

And I wished,

If I could just stop the time.


Shiver went down,

My spine.

And I was high,

As if on wine.


The way you held,

My arm in fear.

And the way you,

Pulled me near.

The child in us,

Went alive.

And sitting on the roof top,

Your soul I dive.

To make you smile,

I felt complete.

It was the best,

Kind of a meet.

Your touch I swear,

Was itself a fantasy.

And I am lost,

In that ecstasy.

That last handshake,

I tried to make it stay.

But life had us different,

And we parted our way.

# 5. If I Go

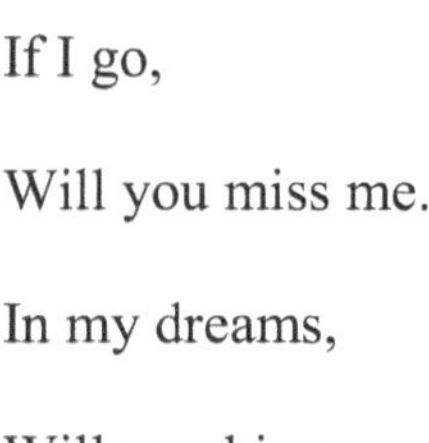

If I go,

Will you miss me.

In my dreams,

Will you kiss me.


If I cry,

Would you make me smile,

And if we meet,

Would you walk an extra mile.


I might be far,

But you'd be in my heart.

Because you are,

My most precious part.


If I go,

Will you find someone replace me.

And if I come back,

Would you be able to face me.

Will you hug me,

In my dreams.

Will you hear,

All my screams.

Will you forgive me,

For going away.

Will you think of me,

On your bed, when you lay.

Will I still be your friend,

Because I can see the end.

Would you let me,

Love you like I do.

And maybe one day,

Would you love me back too.

Would you guide me,

If I go blind.

Would look for me,

And hug me when you find.


Would you think of me,

When you sleep.

Because my love is what,

You can keep.


Would you make me sober,

When I'm high.

Would you save me,

If I die.


Would you blush,

Hearing my name.

Would you miss me,

Hearing to jokes that are lame.

If I go,

Would you fight for us.

Or would we just live,

With the memories of our bus.


I wished a little too much,

To spend with you some starry nights.

But all that is now crushed,

And coming back to 'mights'.


All the memories,

Were yet to be made.

But well,

Our story will now fade.


Will you remember me,

When you see someone alike.

Or will you remember me,

Is you see a couple on a bike.

Will you miss me,

When you need someone to play.

And when you get bored,

To pass your off-day.


Will you miss me,

When the moon shines.

Because I always had a dream,

To make you mine.


If I go,

Please don't cry.

Look up,

N feel me in the sky.

# 6. Friday Night

On a random Friday night,

Sitting under the moonlight.


Hands in hand on roof top,

We both laugh and hop.


Holding our beers up,

We make each other cheer up.


Fighting for the songs,

Trying to make nothing go wrong.


Looking at the skyline,

Under the dim shine.


Playing with your hair,

Was a nostalgic affair.

Your soft sweet touch,

Ahh, I love it so much.


On a random Friday night,

We might meet again.

We might share our hearts,

Walking in the dark windy lane.

# 7. Rain

This season of rain,

It seizes all my pain.


It reminds me of you,

I remember that you enjoyed it too.


The raindrops fall on leaves and they dwell,

In the same way, my heart swells.


There's no one around me,

I wish we played in the rain, only if we could be.


It feels so good in this scorching heat,

As it increases my heartbeat.

I see a couple of dove,

Showcasing their love.


Walking in the ground,

As we did that last night, all around.


As the rain falls on flowers, they bloom,

White flowers on yellow building background as the groom.


I am in love with you, the same as I am in love with this season

of rain,

Seizing all my pain,

Wishing it to happen again,

This season of rain.


This season of rain,

It seizes all my pain...

# 8. Since You Left

Since you left,

I lost interest.

Since you left,

I stopped to trust.


Now the rain,

Doesn't seize the pain.


Now the birds don't fly high,

And I got no tears left to cry.


Now the trees seem lonely,

Because you were the only.


Now the clouds don't seem too far,

But my head and my heart are always at a war.

I miss your touch,

A little too much.


Now my friends,

They don't tease me by your name.

Because you went,

The moment you came.


I tried my luck,

But you didn't give a f*ck.


Since you left,

I haven't slept.

So many secrets,

I have kept.


Now, since you left,

You won't come back.

In my life,

Your presence will always lack.

# 9. Can I Be Him?

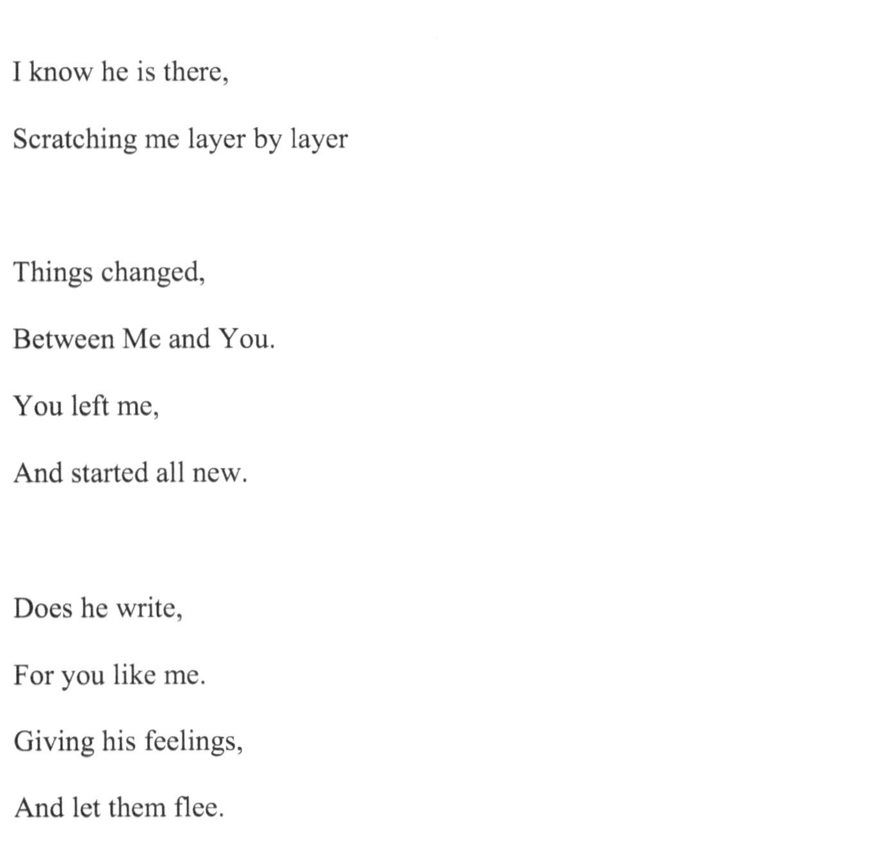

You chose him,

Over me.

He is better.

Really, Is he?


I know he is there,

Scratching me layer by layer


Things changed,

Between Me and You.

You left me,

And started all new.


Does he write,

For you like me.

Giving his feelings,

And let them flee.

Does he sing,

The songs I sang.

And do you sing along,

Holding his hand.


Does he make you laugh,

Like I did.

And do you hug him,

Like a small kid.


He might have got,

Some good hair.

But hey God,

Was it just all fair?


Can I be the one with beard,

With whom you'd be weird.


You broke me,

To choose another.

Did you just forget,

How we loved each other.

Does he make you,

Go to sleep in glory.

Can I be him?

The one in your story.

Does he read,

Not books but your eyes.

And does he know,

You like subs and not fries.

Do you both,

Gaze stars?

Walk barefoot,

And share your scars.

Since you left,

It's all gone.

Can I be him?

Because I won't move on.

33

# 10. Long Walks

Those long walks,

And the illogical talks.


Feeling you by my side,

Watching you go through the emotional tide.


You being shy,

To hold my hand.

Walking barefoot,

On grassland.


Watching the sky,

On my shoulder you lie.


Fighting for the songs,

Which need to play.

Going on roads,

Not knowing the way.

Everything that happened,

Can't be laid with pen on paper.

With your dog's collar in your hand,

You looked dapper.


Now it's all in my mind,

You're lost and I'm unable to find.


I miss the long walks,

And those late night talks.

# 11. Please Don't Say

We're good friends,

But this is all where it ends.

We walk together,

To bring life on track.

But please don't say you love me,

Because I won't be saying it back.


We talk under these stars,

Sharing all our scars.

And you look beautiful,

In the dark black.

But please don't say you love me,

Because I won't be saying it back.


Missing your face,

At this nostalgic place.

Clicking photos to keep,

Memories in my sack.

But please don't say you love me,

Because I won't be saying it back.

Sharing books is a hobby,

I love the way you love my doggy.

Though my heartbeat skips,

When you look at me like that.

But please don't say you love me,

Because I won't be saying it back.

Going away is hard to take,

Both of ours heart will break.

I will miss you,

And our own soundtrack.

But please don't say you love me,

Because I won't be saying it back.

So, please don't say you love me,

Because I might not say it back.

And I won't be able to,

Live my life like that.

Because I know the place,

We are at.

Not being able to love you back.

# 12. I'd Be Lying

I'd be lying,

If I say I'm fine.

I still wish,

You were all mine.


I'd be lying,

If I say I don't miss.

There aren't any moments,

That I cherish.


I'd be lying,

If I say I've moved on.

I can't have these times,

When you're gone.


I'd be lying,

If I say I don't write for you.

I love you,

N I swear it's all true


I'd be lying,

If I say I don't care.

I lost my girl,

And got no one to share.


I'd be lying,

If I say I'm not in a mess.

You look gorgeous,

When you wear that dress.


I'd be lying,

If I say I'm not high.

If I say,

I don't cry.


I'd be lying,

If I say you love me.

We were not,

Just meant to be.

Not meant to be...

# 13. You're Not There

I miss you,

Wish you were here.

But you left me alone,

And now you're not there.


I need you,

To lit up my flare.

I want to hug you,

But you're not there.


To whom should I,

Send my poetry and where.

You were the one,

But now you're not there.


I wake up with,

Things to tell you.

With a craving,

To hear you.


But you're not there,

To listen and argue.

And you're not there,

Well, that's quite true.


To whom should I call,

And ask for a dare.

Wanna tell you about my day,

But you're not there.


To whom should I write letters,

And whom should I call my dear?

I have written many,

But you're not there.


Life goes on,

But I don't feel.

And you're not there,

To make me heal.


Now you've left me,

And gone somewhere.

I want you back,

But now you're not there.

# 14. If He Cries

If he cries with you,

Don't take it easy.

For he won't cry often,

As he is crazy.


He would rather,

Fake a smile.

But will only cry,

Once in a while.


He won't cry,

For his head.

He'd cry his heart out,

And just move ahead.


Feel good,

For he chose you.

Because he's got a world,

To prove he is strong too.


Don't look at him,

With emptiness in your eyes.

For he trusted you,

With his cries.


He won't let that tear,

Get off his eye.

And he won't tell you,

No matter how hard you try.


Don't show him mercy,

Just hug him tight.

And you'll see,

His heart would be alright.


And then you'll see,

He's back to a smile.

Because with you,

It was his once in a while

# 15. Old Friends

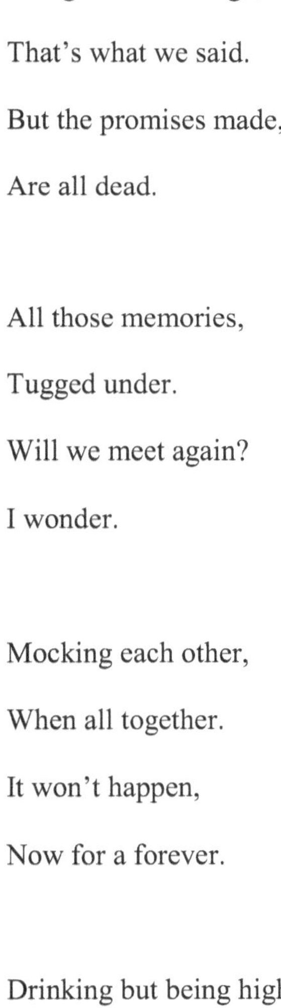

Things won't change,

That's what we said.

But the promises made,

Are all dead.


All those memories,

Tugged under.

Will we meet again?

I wonder.


Mocking each other,

When all together.

It won't happen,

Now for a forever.


Drinking but being high,

Will now be a lie.

Life will change,

Living in college.

But those idiots being the best,

No matter our age.


New jokes and abuses,

Some serious and some hookups.

But old friends hit the mind,

Sitting alone with the coffee cups.


Call you later,

Is what we say.

But later never comes,

As we drift day by day.


New beginning of life,

As the old ends.

Things change when,

Old bastards get new friends.

# 16. Is It Just Me?

Do you see me,

In the night sky?

And talk to the moon,

Asking why?

Do you feel we were meant to be?

Or is it just me?


Do you miss me,

When you hear someone talk like us?

Did you feel like meeting,

Even after all the fuss?

Do you feel lonely even in a party,

Or is it just me?


Do you get drunk,

Sitting on your bed bunk?

Do you see the stars,

And feel the inside wars?

You got alcohol to company,

Or is it just me?


I wish I drove you,

In my car.

And we drove,

Somewhere very far.

Do you wish to flee,

Or is it just me?


Does your heart stop,

When you hear my name?

Or when you hear some jokes

That are as lame?

Do you feel stuck and not free,

Or is it just me?


Do you love me,

Like you love yourself?

And would heal me,

When I'm hurt by myself?

Is there any other 'He',

Or is it just me?

# 17. What We Had

I know it's not right,

But I think of you tonight.


Evening sunsets,

And the dark night skies.

Listening to your voice,

Looking in your eyes.


Reading the same books,

And capturing your funny looks.


Talking the whole night,

Till the sun shines bright.


Being childish,

Like no one cared.

Clicking stupid pictures,

Sharing a bond that no one shared.

I just miss you,

And I can't stop.

Now you're enjoying with friends,

And I'm not.


I do want to see,

You happy,

But I don't want to see ,

You happy without me.


Being so selfish,

And it's bad.

But I don't want somebody,

To have what we had.

# 18. The Dog I Never Had

Walking in the street,

He ran towards me.

Not older than a few months,

He felt quite happy.


Wagging his tail,

And trying to climb.

Here's a poem for you,

That I tried to rhyme.


With his small,

Cute little paw.

I gave him my hand,

Stuck in awe.


I wondered if,

I could take him home.

But he was hers,

So, I walked past alone.


Now I see you again,

Both of you have grown.

None remembering me,

Life changes quick, you've shown.


But you look cute walking,

With his leash in your hand.

Making me happy,

Like a magic wand.

# 19. Would You?

If I ask,

Would you dance?

And give 'Us',

Just one chance.


If I ask you,

To stay and hold on?

Would you relive,

All the moments that are now gone.


Would you cry,

When I'll be crying?

Would you paint,

Both of us in a drawing.


If I ask you,

To fight?

Would you,

Call me up tonight.

If I ask you,

Would you smile?

Just because,

It's been a long while.

If I ask you,

Would you make me calm.

And hide me,

In your arms.

Would you laugh,

Hearing my name?

And would you wait,

Until I came?

If I ask you,

To stop the time.

And forever be mine..

Would you?

# 20. Alright

There used to be a time,

We used to fight.

Now it doesn't,

Really feel alright.


I didn't try hard,

And just let you go.

What shall I do,

I don't really know.


You would be here,

Enjoying the snow.

But now we choose,

The opposite flow.


Dancing in the rain,

Listening to our melodies.

But now, just holding,

On to some memories.


Sitting on the cliff,

Watching the sun set.

An another chance,

That we could get.


Laying on my chest,

Under the moon and stars.

But, now smiling wide,

Hiding both of our scars.

# 21. The Flower In Your Hair

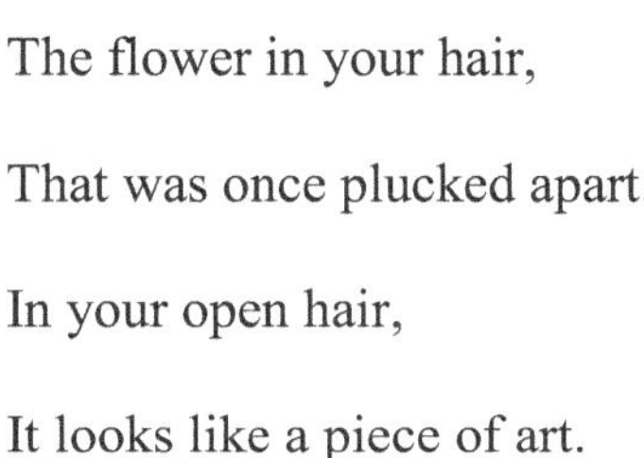

The flower in your hair,

That was once plucked apart.

In your open hair,

It looks like a piece of art.


The light pink rose,

That matched your cheeks.

The way you blushed,

When you used to speak.


The finely curved petals,

In your hair, they slide.

Resembling the way,

You used to smile wide.


The soft velvet texture,

It was so innocent.

Soft as your touch,

For me, it wasn't meant


The sweet fragrance,

Adding up to yours.

Smelled like a garden,

That bloomed near me, and not very far.

# 22. The Cliff

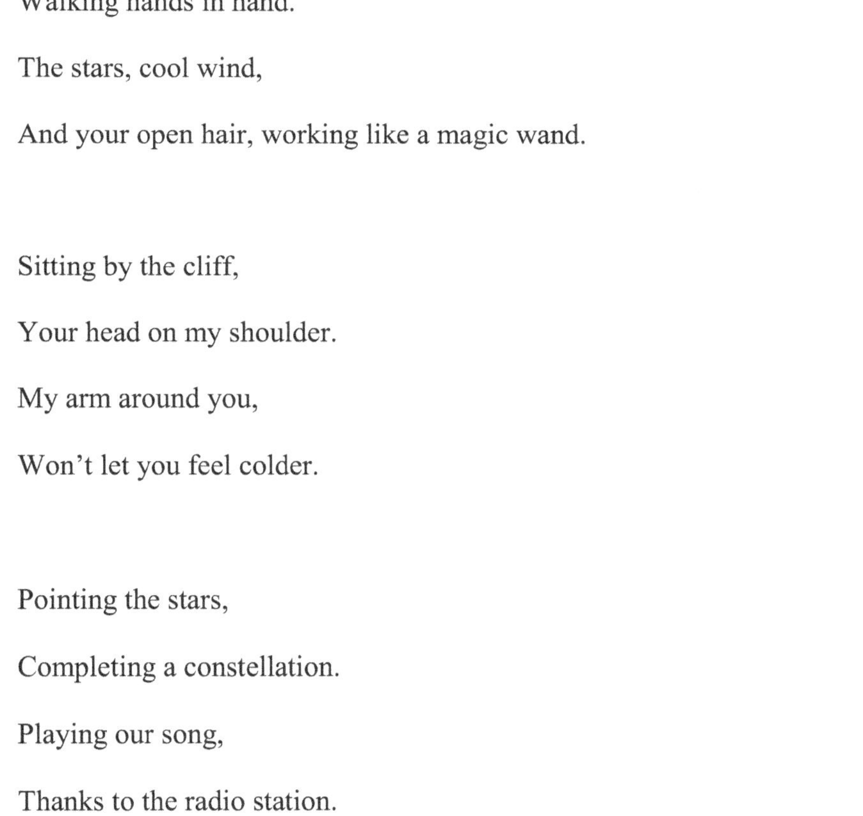

Dark in the night,

Walking hands in hand.

The stars, cool wind,

And your open hair, working like a magic wand.


Sitting by the cliff,

Your head on my shoulder.

My arm around you,

Won't let you feel colder.


Pointing the stars,

Completing a constellation.

Playing our song,

Thanks to the radio station.


Hands up in the air,

We enjoy the lights.

Because maybe we knew,

There won't be any other nights.


Now I sit alone,

On the same cliff.

Watching the stars,

But my heart is a little stiff.


I look at the same stars,

Making the constellation.

But the songs have changed,

At the old radio station.


The night doesn't feel,

Like it felt before.

Because you aren't there,

By my side anymore.


Now, dark in the night,

Walking all alone.

Cool breeze, but empty hands,

And the time that has flown.

# 23. A Girl In The Coffee Shop

Sitting on the table,

Looking into the screen.

Your lips smiled wide,

Looking so happy.


A scrunchie holding up,

All your messy hair.

Wide glasses on your face,

That you hardly wear.


Sipping up your coffee,

Leaving a mark around your lips.

And then cleaning it,

With those soft fingertips.


Only if we locked our eyes,

Just in there.

It'd be the two of us,

In our maiden glare.

68

And you'd be the pretty girl,

In the coffee shop.

I'd look at whom

Looking at the desktop.

# 24. How Could Someone Not Like

# Rain

How could someone,

Not like rain.

When it soothes,

All his veins.


When it makes you,

Feel like heaven.

And makes your heart,

And head balance even.


When it makes you,

Lose control and let go.

The feelings you can't,

Just throw.

When the rain drops,

Kiss your face.

And the water takes,

You in its embrace.


Raindrops being cold,

But you still feel the warmness.

Warmth of the water,

Hugging you like a harness.


When it makes your head,

Shut down and go around.

And makes your heart beat,

Let it feel and pound.


When it makes you write,

And pen down your words.

And connect you to people,

From different worlds.



How could someone,

Just not like the rain.

When it makes you smile,

And seizes all your pain...

When it makes you sing,

Your favourite songs again...

# 25. A Drive Alone

Our song on the radio,

I drive all alone.

Sun setting on the beach side,

But how far we've grown.


A hand on the wheel,

Cruising high speed.

Lyrics tear me down,

Not knowing where I lead.


It goes a little blurry,

And I feel you by my side.

Looking at the sky,

All open wide.


I'd stop by the beach side,

Watching the water waves.

And I'd read my poems,

Reliving the old days.


I smile wide,

With a tear in my eye.

With that feeling of yours,

I feel so damn high.


Would you ever know,

That I drove that way.

Feeling you near me,

Even when you went away.